Painting My Way to Success:
A "Paint and Sip" Business:
Your questions answered.

By Anne Ruemler

ISBN: 978=1514622155

INTRODUCTION

Hi, my name is Anne Ruemler. I have had an overwhelming response to my e-book "Painting My Way to Success: How I started my very own "Paint and Sip" business for under $1000. So, I thought I would compile some of my emails from readers that were either planning on starting their own paint and sip business, or were already actively running a similar business but had questions or comments.

I will remove all personal information from these emails, but I will keep as much of my original responses as possible. Some of these emails may seem to repeat themselves, but all the information and questions are very relevant to this business so I am leaving them intact.

I have received calls, Facebook messages and emails from around the world. It is so amazing to me that my little book has touched so many people and given several a new start at owning their very own business. I enjoy all my correspondences. I have connected with people through this business I would have never thought possible. I wish all the wonderful ladies and one gentleman that I have spoken to over the past year the VERY BEST of luck with their businesses. You have filled my heart with your kind words about my e-book and strengthened my faith in this business.

I have since sold my business to one of my artists. My reason was simple, I am a business woman and I was presented an offer to expand into Real Estate that was simply too good to pass up, and the requirements on my time became more restrictive. My contract with Fort Knox was amazing and I was so happy to have had the chance to host a Spirited Canvases painting party with the Post Commanding Brigadier General, an honor I have treasured ever since.

I am still available through email and Facebook. I will continue to respond to fellow entrepreneurs by answering questions or with words of encouragement. I have more than 22 years' experience in customer service and leading teams, so if you are stuck or do not know how to "handle" an issue. I may be able to help.

I will start with the very first email I received after my book was published. I was so excited to see someone not only read my book and loved it, but they had questions and felt comfortable enough with me to write. That was so heartwarming. Every email that I have received I put everything I have into responding back. I love teaching and training. Knowledge is power and I love sharing both!

READERS QUESTIONS AND E-MAILS

QUESTION #1:

Dear Anne,

Thank you for writing "Painting My Way to Success". I found the book to be very encouraging. Also, I was happy to find the book full of pertinent and useful information regarding the basics for starting one's own "Paint & Sip".

Thanks to you sharing your wisdom and knowledge with the world. I am now confident with my decision to run with the idea and am now ready to begin working on a business plan. Only time will tell whether the UK is ready for an American to "introduce" them to the P&S industry or not. Stay tuned!!

In the meantime, if I have questions or ideas regarding P&S and want to bounce them off a like-minded individual, would you be willing to answer my questions via email? If not, is there anyone you would recommend I connect with for a bit of support or encouragement now and again?

I look forward to hearing back from you at your earliest convenience.

Kind regards,

ANNE'S RESPONSE:

Good Afternoon,
I am so glad you contacted me. Although I'm sure there are many differences from the United States and UK. This business is very adaptable and tons of fun.
It is a very exciting business and will take you places you never thought possible. I have met some truly wonderful people and am looking forward to meeting many more.. Good Luck and please do not hesitate to reach out to me with any questions or concerns....
Sincerely,
Anne Ruemler
Spirited Canvases of Elizabethtown

QUESTION #2:

Anne, Thank you again for your encouragement.

The UK is going to be an interesting place to begin the business, but life's an adventure and I'm up for the challenge.

If you had to start Spirited Canvases all over again, is there anything you would do differently?   If so, please explain.

It must have been very disheartening to experience going through the motions of setting up for an event only to tear down a short time later. What advice do you have for someone wanting to avoid the same pitfalls?

Regards,

ANNE'S RESPONSE:

I have spent the last few hours at an event on Fort Knox Ky. Check out my Facebook page. I posted pictures...

I will say that I have had my share of "No Shows" at events. It is a very deflating feeling to pack up with your head hung low and your pockets empty...
Because of this I NO LONGER set up public events. I used to take a painting and an easel to a local restaurant and make flyers with all my information on it. THIS IS STILL A GREAT WAY TO GET YOUR INFORMATION OUT THERE...I honestly just booked a private party from a lady who picked up a flyer at a restaurant, but did not want to attend that event..
I still host parties at popular local restaurants, but they are not open to the public.

All my events are now "private" parties or fundraisers and I now require a small deposit at time of booking. I charge $50 for children's parties and $35 for adult parties. It's not a lot of money, but if they cancel you're not out everything...
I have rescheduled a lot of parties. I always push to move dates rather than canceling the event altogether. I once had a Jimmy Buffet party rescheduled 4 months later... and it turned out to be an AWESOME event with our local American Legion.
I hope this has helped you. You will have great events and you will have Okay events. I have not had a BAD event yet... no shows don't count ;)
Are you military living overseas?? If you are get with your local MWR. They can get you under contract to paint for our soldiers and families. Very rewarding. My husband is retired military. So is my Dad....

Good Luck and keep me posted... I'm so excited to have a fellow P &S owner to mentor.

GOOD NIGHT....
Anne Ruemler

QUESTION #3:

I have officially visited and liked your Spirited Canvases page. :0)

Who is your easel supplier? I wonder if I can find that style on Amazon.Intl. I've never seen easels in that shape before.

Speaking of 'never', I must share a little secret. I've never even been to a P&S event before. It's the biggest reason I am so nervous about this whole venture and unsure of exactly how to go about everything. I am grateful you are a willing mentor. Thank you.

No, we are not military.

Thank you for all you and your family do to keep America safe and secure!! I can't even begin to imagine the state of things if we were without our troops. May God richly bless you and your family in all you do.

I am finally feeling settled and am happily focused on writing my business plan. Did you write a business plan?

Take care!

ANNE'S RESPONSE:

Hello....
There are quite a few tabletop easels available on Amazon. The small black easels are pretty sturdy. Don't spend more than $10 USD per easel. Just start with10 easels ... then build up to 20....
Don't be afraid to get out there and introduce yourself. You don't have to book events yet. Maybe just pass out flyers and start building relationships with Managers and Owners.
As my husband says....."Just throw your hat over the fence!"

I did not write a formal business plan. I bought all inventory with my savings. I did write weekly goals for myself. I started my Monday with a strict marketing plan for the week.

Monday: Visit 5 new Restaurants.

Tuesdays: Follow up with last weeks' Restaurants. (Try to get at least 1 new booking)

Wednesday: Research 5 local children's groups that might need a fundraiser and contact them.

Thursday: Inventory paint, canvas and other supplies for the weekend events planned.

Friday: Call/Email special pricing offers to past customers. Let them know about any future events.

Saturday: Pass out flyers to anyone you come across throughout the day. I would go to local festivals, the movies and the Farmer's Market on Saturday mornings. Hope this helped.

QUESTION #4:

Hello Anne,

Did you receive the email w/logo idea et al? What do you think? Any advice?

How are your shows going this week?

May I please ask, how many events do you average a month and how many people per event do you average? Finally, how long did it take to you to develop consistent numbers of events and # of people in attendance?

Thanks,

ANNE'S RESPONSE:

Good Evening,
I really like your logo.. I think it is creative, but do u like it? This is your brand... can u see yourself married to this logo? Just a thought. With my logo. I use a wine glass. I have been asked if I provide wine. Of course I do not... Just another thought....

I started my mobile business 1 year ago... I started with 2 to 3 events a month, but I also worked 45 hours a week as a retail manager.
Since working my business full time I average 6 to 9 events a month.
EVERY Saturday is booked and most Friday's for the next 3 months.
I even have a Cheerleaders of Central Kentucky fundraiser booked in January!!
My average events for fundraisers depends really. Small boosters clubs from schools can be 10 to 15. I had an elementary PTA fundraiser that was 116 people!!! I split it into 2 classes!!! I think it's safe to say 4 to 8 people average....to start....you'll build from there.
I'm sure your area is much larger. My town is 38000 population...
Once I joined my local chamber of Commerce my phone started ringing. If you have anything like that or local "family" website to advertise in. It really helps get your name out.
Do yourself a favor and get a deposit for any private party... that will hopefully keep people from cancelling...

Hope that answered your questions...
Talk to you soon....
Anne
PS
I have 2 private birthday parties this week.... and a face painting event!!

QUESTION #5:

Hello Anne,

Yes, thank you, you have answered my questions. You've made great points regarding my logo. I am looking at business name and logo/branding in a different light now.

I am no longer keen on the name I chose. "RI" served its purpose in getting me to begin writing my business plan, so all is not lost. Back to the drawing board. :0)

1) When you advertise for /hire artists, what wording, (specifications or parameters) do you give them to get across the type of paintings you want created since full-on masterpieces are not going to work? Do u limit number of colors in paintings or something?

2) Do you hold auditions (ie here's a spec and small canvas, be ready to teach what you paint in 1/2hr during your interview?) or do you just look through portfolios? Where do u find your artists? Word of mouth? I live near Reading University and plan to advertise there.

3) As far as the artwork... Who owns copyrights? Do you state in your artist contract that whatever paintings are created for use on the site to promote business or hold events belongs to the company or do you not worry about that sort of thing? (Just thinking of copyright laws. Would hate for an artist to leave and take w/them a popular painting or say it's no longer avail for use... Or even go so far as to sue for copyright infringement if they become a diva or something.)

4) In an earlier email, you mentioned something about artists not painting until the night before. That statement made me think, 'Aren't the paintings already finished and posted on your calendar on the website in advance?' If so, I don't quite understand.... Where does the requirement of painting, which is sometimes left until the night before, come into play?

How exciting that you've started booking for Jan already! Wow! A 116 person fundraising event into two groups... How many assistants did you need for your artist during those sessions?

I hope your 2 private parties and Face Painting event have gone well. What made you add Face Painting to your menu of services? Are you teaching people to face paint or are you hiring self out as face painter?

Must get back to the drawing board...
Take care, hope to hear from you soon.

ANNE'S RESPONSE:

Good Morning,
   I was out late last night for a fundraiser. Had a blast. We were expecting 8, and 14 showed up. Very common.
      Okay, when I recruit artists I am very casual. We are selling the experience not so much the art. I look for someone who has taught, a teacher or a nurse maybe even someone with experience leading teams. They MUST be relaxed, fun and able to connect with middle aged women. That will be most of your "Painters".
   I have never worked with a male artist. Although I do have a fantastic pastel artist that is willing to teach classes for me. I personally think he is AMAZING and WAY too advanced for my painters. I am thinking about stretching my wings and allowing him to teach some ADVANCED classes. The customer would pay for all the materials. That stuff is pricey.
      I advertise using my Facebook and website. A simple "Shout Out" something simple.
"Hey fellow artists. Spirited Canvases of Elizabethtown is growing. We are looking for a new artist to create new fun light hearted art work and teach classes. These are mostly evening and weekend events. Times and days very. If you are interested please message me and we'll set up an interview time."
   At the "Interview" I ask for background. Have they taught? Look at some of their work. Did they bring some with them? Even

pictures are fine. DO I LIKE THEM?!! If I don't connect with them…. My painters will not connect with them.

The paintings MUST be simple. If they can complete it within 30-40 minutes it should work. Stay with trends. Americans love the holidays. We are painting pumpkins and working on a few Halloween. You can find a lot of inspiration visiting other Paint and Sip websites. Just change that painting 30% or you could get a letter from an attorney… No fun.

There are several different paint and sip businesses that have locations all around the US and each location will have some local artwork. These are simple paintings that are very popular. I choose the paintings with the fewest colors. Maybe 8 different colors max. I have taken 15 different colors to an event. Sometimes a painter will want a different color. I do allow this on small classes. It's just good customer service.

I just hired an artist this week that was a painter. She has attended 4 of my events on Fort Knox and answered my posting. Of course I knew her art style because I had seen her work on several different pieces. That was an easy hire. I interviewed her and was delighted to learn that she was an English major and a professional writer. She had also had been a full time substitute teacher for several years and of course I liked her. Just perfect!!

I like to walk around my painters as my instructor is instructing and praise their works of art. If I see a great painting I announce that I just found our next instructor!! Everyone gets a kick out of that. But it does work.

I think your college students would be PERFECT!! I would definitely hang postings announcing open interviews with the art department.

Now the copy right issue. My artist are technically recreating simple work. Nothing has been copy written but I ask the artist if they want to keep their work anyway. I usually am told that I can keep it. I separated from an artist several months ago but she did not want her work back. I was very happy. They were really good. I still use them for advertising.

When I first started Spirited Canvases I had commissioned a great artist. She was so much fun. I still stay in contact with her and

LOVE her simple style. She would produce a "draft" of a painting. I would post that painting as advertisement. The idea was that within 48 hour I would have the completed painting so I could take it to the Venue and post it at the door along with my flyers. After several times of her running into the class at starting time with painting in hand I stopped scheduling her.

The last straw was when she was filling in for another artist whose mother had passed away. She had several days to produce her version of the painting, but asked me to print a picture of the painting just 30 minutes before class so she could teach it!!

Thank goodness she pulled that class out of her "Butt" and everyone had a great time.

I now require my artist to have the work completed within 72 hours. I have them texted me a picture that I post on my website and Facebook page.

Our face painting was inspired by a local lady who does these amazing face painting events. She is the ONLY face painter in the area. Well, she is commissioned out by local businesses for $700.00 an event!! Me, being a business owner I had to jump on that!! I personally am only able to paint simple styles. I leave the fancy butterflies and tigers to my artists.

I posted "We are now face painting!! Call or message me to book your face painter now!!" I received 6 requests within 2 weeks.

There are a lot of summer and fall festivals in my area, so we set up a table and paint faces for $3.00 a child. I have cleared $300.00 an event. What a great way to get your name out there too!! I pass out my flyers all day!! My artist will start by painting a few lucky kids for free then send them out to spread the word!! It works EVERY TIME!!

Okay, I believe I have covered everything.

Anne

Spirited Canvases

QUESTION #6:

Hi Anne,

I recently bought and read your kindle book on starting a paint & sip business.
First of all, thank you very much for writing a very informative book with no-fluff. You got straight to the point and it was a very quick read, which I like. :)
I'm in NYC and actually enjoy painting myself although I really don't think it's something I could teach, as it's just a hobby. This leads me to a few questions I had that I hope you can help me out with...

1. How and/or where did you find your painting teachers?
2. How are the paintings for your classes selected? Are they originals that
your painting teacher paints beforehand or do you find a pictures online you like or some other method?
3. How far in advance do you plan for picture selections, in other words, to setup your online calendar, are all pictures selected and uploaded to your calendar a month in advance so attendees know what they'll be working on?

I think that's it but I'm sure something else will come up later. Thank you dearly for taking the time to answer.

Sincerely,

ANNE'S RESPONSE:

Good Evening. Thank you so much for contacting me. I just happened to find your email in my spam folder. I'm so glad I looked before hitting the little trash can icon.
THANKS for the kind words. Please leave a review on my book. As you can tell I'm not an author...but I am a business women ...

I have thought about each of your questions and think I have some answers for you…

1. I met my artists at Michaels Crafts. I was an Assistant Store Manager there for a couple years. Great place to meet artists. Retired Art teachers are also great. Believe it or not Nurses are also great teachers. They have to be light hearted and fun too. Just a thought.

2. I choose paintings that are popular. With my strong retail background I tend to focus on seasonal paintings. They just sell. We are painting fall paintings now. I do have on occasion a request, but I do not "Copy" another artist painting. The law requires at least a 30% change in artwork. This keeps me within the legal copyright range. I have been threatened with attorneys before for posting another artists artwork just to show how cute it was. NOT FUN!! So always change color or add a little **extra** to any painting. You can get a lot of inspiration from other Paint and Sip companies. I have a very good artist that likes to create original, but once in a while we will alter someone else's work because it was requested from a customer. Just remember the 30% rule. Pinterest.com is also a great website to find paintings on. Just KEEP THEM SIMPLE.

3. As far as my calendar is concerned I like to fill as I book events. I also like to post "Book your private party here" on available dates. I think if I fill my calendar with paintings and random classes with no paying customers "just to fill a calendar" can deter someone from calling to book…simply because they think I'm already booked.. I see nothing wrong with having open dates on your calendar. I VERY rarely book an event within 3 weeks. So I guess you can say that I fill my calendar a month in advance. My business itself is in transition. I am leaving one artist and gaining another. One of my current Artists also has her own paint and sip business and has stepped on my toes a lot lately by contacting MY customers and soliciting to them. NOT COOL!! So I have initiated a COOL DOWN period. I will still work with her, but on MY terms. Another lesson I had to learn I guess.

I hope this has helped... I am also working with a new Paint and Sip business owner in the UK!! I just LOVE this business and am so excited to help. Please keep me informed. Have you chosen a name and LOGO yet? VERY important.

Good Luck and Happy Painting!!
Anne

QUESTION #7:

Anne... so glad you didn't trash your mail.
Anyway, thanks for getting back. I have not chosen name and logo yet. I'm
sort of in research phase: reading, pricing everything out, etc.

Your answers are very helpful. That's interesting that you mentioned nurses as teachers. I would have never thought of this. I assumed that any teacher would need a painting background, someone who has taught before, especially beginners.

A friend of mine recommend her artist friend to me and we've been talking. She's a very experienced painter and teacher. She's know how much she wants to be paid for each class but is flexible. When I mentioned creating paintings for the classes she said this is an additional expense ($100 per painting is common according to her). What's your take on this? Do you pay your teachers in addition to teaching class to create the art work? Do you ever repeat paintings for later classes, for instance, do you use certain paintings in other months. I don't know if that would turn-off customers so I'm curious because it would cut down on new, original paintings for each class.

Also do you collaborate with painter for original artwork for class? The creating of the painting, selecting, coming up with what to paint seems the most daunting to me right now. I want to make it a seamless process for whomever I'm working with.

Any insight is appreciated. I will leave you a review of your book too. Glad you mentioned it because I didn't think about it.

Best

ANNE'S RESPONSE:

Okay. Let's get right to it. I DO NOT pay my artist for a painting, and that IS NOT common in this business. We are selling the experience NOT art instruction. This is a social event not an art class. I am so glad to hear that I helped you. I am working with a very forceful Artist right now. It is very difficult to regain "control" of your own business when you have a demanding artist. I am sure your artist's work is beautiful but unless you are truly interested in teaching ART, she may not be the one for your ENTERTAINMENT business.

You need to look for a light hearted artist that can paint a simple beginners painting and instruct simple beginner techniques. One of my current artists does have a Master's in Education, and, I also have a retired English Lit teacher, however, they are fun people who can paint too. .. The only thing I do provide is simple 16X20 1/4 stretched canvases. I ask them NOT to use fancy expensive paints... although they will try then complain about my selection. Oh WELL. As the OWNER we have to watch our cost.
I have one artist that WILL NOT use my inexpensive brushes. She brings her own. That is on her. But I always have mine available.
Artist can be eccentric. You just have to get used to that, but you DO NOT have to keep them if they are costing you money.

I do reuse paintings. I have a beach scene painting that is easy and very pretty. We have painted that one painting five times since February!! I will get my paintings from simple web searches. Check other paint and sip businesses websites just make sure to alter it 30%.

Fleur Di Les are very popular. I can email a few of my popular ones. Let your artist create also. Just keep it simple. NO MORE than 6 or 7 colors. That will also get expensive.

   Okay, think I covered everything.

I will send you another email with several of my paintings. Check out my Facebook page and website. I have some cool pictures on there too.

Talk to you later!!
Anne

QUESTION #8:

Thanks again for getting back to me. Well, I'd love to schedule a 30 min call with you. Not sure how long I'll need but figure I'd start with 30 minutes.

I'm compiling a list of questions now. I know its last minute but does this Fri work.

If not, Sat or Sun (if you work on wknds) or next Mon is good too.

Ok, let me know what works for you. Looking forward to chatting. :)

ANNE'S RESPONSE:

Good Afternoon,

   Yes, I would be available for coaching calls. I love this business and very much enjoy teaching others. Let me know when you are available and I will lock my teenagers, hubby and cats out of my office and focus on your questions. My current rates are $35 per hour or $20 for 30 minutes. I can accept payment through my website, or take it over the phone. Just let me know and I will schedule it on my calendar. I look forward to hearing from you soon. I am on my way to a street festival downtown to pass out a few flyers with my hubby.

Anne Ruemler

QUESTION #9:

Hi Anne,

My name's D. I live in Southern CA and plan to start a Paint and Sip business in the coming months. It won't be a mobile business, so it's a little different than what you created, but I think the concepts are universal. Anyway, I have just a few questions for you (may have some more later and really do appreciate your time):

How profitable was the business?

Did you ever meet or exceed your annual goal of $50k?

Did you end up only paying artists' 25% commission?

How many artists did you need and what's the best way to find them?

Why did you turn your company over?

Any other insight would be awesome...

Thanks again,

D

ANNE'S RESPONSE:

Good Evening,
I am so excited to talk with you.

1. I paid my Artist 33% of my sales. This was a HANDSOME paycheck for the instructor. The motive behind this pay scale was to encourage my artist to BUILD her class size. This did not happen. I did eventually add another artist which I paid $25 per hour. I felt this was a fair pay rate.
2. I was at every class. I would assist in handing out paint, clean water and fresh plates. It is a bit like waiting tables at a restaurant, but it gave me the opportunity to get close to my customer and build that relationship. My Instructor could easily manage a class of up to 30 with my assistance. If there was more than 30 I would bring along a supporting instructor and pay $25 per hour to assist.
3. College students can be a great place to recruit Artist. Even retired teachers. Go to other Paint and Sip events scope them out. One of my artist was a student at several of my classes. I also posted an "advertisement" on my Facebook page. I had several replies and I interviewed 3 candidates.
4. The profitability of Spirited Canvases was slow to start. ALL of my advertising was word of mouth, door knocking and Facebook. I put very little money in advertising and I only worked one event per week. I sold my business in September and YTD sales were $14,000 with 4 more months in the year. I feel confident that my business would have continued to grow, but did not see it making more than $30,000 a year in my small town. The business I sold to is still very active in the school systems and on Fort Knox where they host parties for our military and their families.
5. As I mentioned in my book I am NOT an Artist. I love building and running businesses. I created and promoted a thriving small business and was approached by an Artist to buy me out with a handsome payout. So… I sold my inventory and contracts with the military to her.

I hope this has helped. If I could do it again….. I would start the Artist at $25 per hour. I think paying my instructor such a high rate stunted the growth of my business. I should have thought out a strong marketing plan with that money instead of handing it to her (the 33%).

Keep the events FUN!! ENTERTAINING!! You do not want an artist that barks orders and wants it run like a classroom, it's an entertainment business not a class room!!

I love sharing ideas and information.
Let me know how you are doing. I mentor 2 other owners 1 in New York and even 1 in the UK.
Good Luck.
Anne Ruemler

QUESTION #10:

Hi Anne,

What was the main type of person you usually saw at your events, e.g. age, gender, etc? Was there a target audience you always noticed?

Thanks again!

ANNE'S RESPONSE:

90% women. Mother and Daughter was very common. Women in their 40's, the empty nesters, were most common. Although, I had a school schedule a "Mommy and Me" event around Mother's Day. I had 40 painters!

Talk to you soon,

Anne

QUESTION #11:

Wow. Thank you so much for the thoughtful reply and all the good information. I would love to remain in contact with you, as I don't want to reinvent the wheel! A quick question for the time being... when you paid an hourly wage, did that mean you had to deal with things that come with having an employee as opposed to contracting an artist? Would it have made sense to drop the 33% of that days sales to say 25% or is best to have a set hourly wage?

Thanks again!

D

ANNE'S RESPONSE:

I offered $75 per class. Three hours was a normal class, 30 min to set up, 2 hour painting then 30 minutes to clean up.
   They are considered independent contractors. I would give them a 1099 at the end of the year. Quite a bit easier than taking out taxes on them.
Hope that helps... get a hold of a good book keeper. They will help u with your state laws
Keep in touch,
Anne

ANNE'S Response to email. Cannot find original email:

I am finally slowing down enough to write. I have been so busy and I do apologize for the long wait...

Okay, I am a no nonsense type of person so let's get to your questions.....

1. Hiring an artist..... Remember your customer base is most likely older women that have NEVER painted before. So your artist must be able to teach the beginner. A simple painting like a beach scene or a tree. Your main goal is to have ALL clients COMPLETE their painting. If it is too difficult you will frustrate your customer and overwhelm them.

2. To get inspiration I looked at other Paint and Sip websites. You MUST NOT copy their work, change it up 30% or more to stay out of copyright trouble. You are welcomed to browse through my Facebook page for inspiration. NOTHING is copy written on my page and are all originals. Pinterest can also give you great BEGINNER ideas.

3. Your artist MUST BE FUN!! You are creating ENTERTAINMENT not an art class. You can always offer private lessons for the more advanced students. College students are awesome instructors.... retired teachers are also great. One of my artist was a retired nurse.

4. I used Michael's craft smart acrylic paints. Hobby Lobby also carries a similar brand. They are the 2oz bottle for crafts. I think they were .69 a bottle. Very cheap..

5. I started with the primary colors. You will need extra white and black to blend colors. I bought 1/2 gallon jugs of white and black. I think I started with $100 in paints.

6. I used foam disposable plates always. I did not want to wash dishes after an event. Dollar General has like 200 plates for 5.00. Many painters will want several plates. They get weird if their paint touches and think that the paint is no longer usable.

7. The big tote from Home Depot I felt came in useful, but the lady I sold my business to felt they were too heavy for her and chose to make several trips and just carry everything in the building. That is your choice.

8. No Shows: You have people call you and tell you they will be at an event and then not show. This is reality. At the end of my business I was requiring a $50 deposit on all

private events. This was NON refundable. You will just have to work out a policy that works for you. I also had a merchant account where I could run credit cards over the phone.

9. IRS and taxes. If you get military contracts like I did you will receive a 1099 at the end of the year. PLEASE get a book keeper to walk you through how to pay your quarterly taxes. It gets VERY confusing.

I hope this helps. I am very excited for you. I think your idea on a press release and free party sounds amazing!! It will take several months to build your brand. It is such a great experience at the end of each class to have that group picture!! I called it the "Magical Moment!"
Good luck and PLEASE let me know how it is going!!
Anne Ruemler

QUESTION #12:

Hello, my name is C and I am interested in starting my own sip and paint business. I just read your book and I have a few questions I hope you can help me with.
How do you get the paintings that you offer in your classes? I read somewhere there is a book of paintings with step by step instructions but I can't find it.
Have you heard of this book?
When customers pay with credit card can they just sign tablet?
Do you need a printer for a receipt?
Thanks for any help you can give me.

ANNE'S RESPONSE:

Good Evening!!

I loved my "Paint and Sip" business!! I hope you have as much fun as I had… Now let's get to your questions…..

1. I did not use a book for inspiration or instruction on my paintings. My artist would create a SIMPLE BEGINNER painting that could be completed within a 2 hour period. I would browse other paint and sip websites and then change a painting at least 30% so not to break any copyright laws. I also asked friends and family what they liked. TREES and BEACH scenes were my most popular. Kentucky is famous for the Kentucky Derby and bourbon whiskey. So I would also paint derby hats and bourbon bottles on canvas.
2. My merchant account did not require a signature. It will depend on the bank that you use to process your credit cards. Yes, some will require a signature. I did not print a receipt at time of payment. My merchant account allowed me to email and text message receipts that worked out very well.

I hope this has helped. Please review my book on amazon. I love to hear everyone's feedback. I truly wish you the best of luck. If you have any more questions just email me and I will gladly answer them.
Anne Ruemler

QUESTION #13:

Good day Ms. Ruemler,

I am DT soon to be paint party entrepreneur. I have purchased your book--Painting My Way to Success. It is exactly the information I needed to start the paint party biz. Like yourself I'd rather be a mobile business less overhead. I was hoping for a supply list. It seems as if the prices you have listed are retail. If you are willing please send me a list of suppliers. I am looking for the most cost effective products being offered. I also like to know if your artists create all the works of art or you have catalog to choose artwork. I am hoping to utilize this business as a fundraiser and events for kids-birthday parties, girl-scout troops etc. One more question-do your clients trace paintings and then color? I saw a company that offers this type of model more for DIY. I want to thank you for having the courage to write the book because I did not see anything else like it on Amazon. Your book of information is much appreciated. Thanks in advance for your assistance.

DT

ANNE'S RESPONSE:

Good Morning from Kentucky....
    I am so glad to hear from you... I love "talking" to other entrepreneurs.

I purchased my paint supplies... Easels, canvas, paint and brushes at Michaels crafts for a couple different reasons...

1. I worked there as a Manager so I was able to use my discount and I always knew when the KILLER sales were on canvas.

2. Most important reason. I didn't pay shipping... I found that with whole sale you may be required to purchase in BULK. I didn't always need to buy in bulk. Just a few easels or 10 canvases would be all I needed. www.Jerrysartarama.com is a very good site for discounted items. One of my artist bought all of her paint brushes there. She hated to use mine...

I have to be honest my artist would surf the competition for inspiration... MAKE SURE you change any painting at least 30% so you are not breaking any copyright laws. I found things like Trees, beaches and lighthouses were very popular. Also seasonal paintings. We love to paint Derby Hats and Bourbon bottles here in Kentucky.

With the Derby Hat painting and a Fleur Dis Le my artist did trace the painting with pencil. It worked out well. Most painters are BRAND NEW and have never painted a day in their life. You DO NOT want them frustrated. I believe if the painting is SIMPLE you should never have a bad event. Beach scenes and trees are so simple though Palm trees can be a little tricky.

This business is really about FUN not necessarily about painting or drinking. Keep it light and make sure your artist is fun and can teach. The Art school would be a GREAT place to recruit a teacher, but it's not art instruction. It's a painting EVENT. Big difference.

Please take a few minutes and review my book on amazon. I'd really appreciate it, and please keep in touch. I'd love to know how it's coming along.

Anne Ruemler

Spirited Canvases

"Where canvas, paint and good people come together."

QUESTION #14:

Anne,

I am a full-time stay at home mom with 3 children so I'm running everything from my kitchen table. I am an artist so I create all original work or take my clients ideas and create for them for my events. It's a lot of work to build up my "stock paintings" right now but well worth to be unique because I realized there are at least 2 other corporate businesses in my area doing this-big competition!

I realized I have done quite a few things right and am feeling encouraged after reading your book! I only have 12 easels right now and have had 3 successful events! I am only using Facebook because

I can't afford a website yet. It's also just me painting, booking, set up and instruction at events- I can't afford employees so I'm flying solo!

I absolutely love this business so far.
You're an inspiration,
Thanks again,
SL

ANNE'S RESPONSE:

Wow! It sounds like you are doing it right!! Every event will be an opportunity to meet new people and make new contacts. Remember to get names, phone numbers and email addresses for later use. Ask where they work or what they are involved in ie: church, girl scouts ect. If you branch out to FACE PAINTING. You can really get out there. We have a local face painter that has PRINCESS PARTIES and SUPER HERO parties. The artists dresses up like the characters and they are BOOKED! Just another idea. PLEASE keep in contact. I truly miss hosting the events.....but I am still doing what I was born to do... That is teach women how to start a business!! GOOD LUCK!!
Anne Ruemler
Spirited Canvases
"Where paint, canvas and good people come together!"

QUESTION #15:

Hello Anne,

My name is R. I got your email address from your Facebook page and I'm hoping you might answer about your business. I live in Lake Stevens, WA and I'm interested in starting a paint and sip business. I'm a preschool teacher and I'm thinking of hosting private events over the summer to make some extra money. If it goes well, I'd be interested in opening a studio someday (whenever chasing 4 year-olds all day gets to be too much lol). I read your book and I really loved it. I like how straight forward it's written and that you included every step and detail. It's made this idea seem very possible for me.

My only question so far is about working with artists. I was wondering what kind of rights you retain to original artwork created by an artist for your company? If an artist stops working for you do you discontinue using their original artwork or do you have some kind of contract with artists giving you intellectual property rights to artwork created for you company? It just seems like it might be hard to keep artists on long term, or at least it can't be guaranteed, and it seems like a shame to be removing paintings from your selection. Do you have any other contract with your artists, like in regards to their obligation to your company?

I'd appreciate any advice you can give me.
Thanks, R

ANNE'S RESPONSE:

Good Evening R,

Sorry it took me so long to get back with you. I had a hot water heater and sump pump emergency this week. Man, What a mess...

Let's hop into your question..... To Copy Right....Or Not to Copy Right? Now that is your question...
I personally did not retain any rights to my Artist paintings. I wanted a SIMPLE painting that could be completed within 2 hours by a NON Painter. Someone who never painted before, so that being said our paintings were very elementary. A beach scene, trees or a cute owl. These were the types of paintings we did.

I noticed that if the painting was difficult it would STRESS the painter and they would stop painting. I NEEDED EVERYONE to take home a COMPLETED painting at the end of the event.

My events were FUN and silly. I would walk around the painters and gab and compliment their work. I really tried to stay away from a formal sitting. If someone wanted more Formal instruction they could book a PRIVATE session. This is why I never bothered with the copy right. Honestly our paintings were just so simple I didn't see the need to spend the money or resources on copy righting.

It can be hard to retain artists sometimes. Some show up late, some cannot teach, some are NO FUN. When an Artist left Spirited Canvases it was understood that I kept the artwork. Since none of their artwork was copy written anyway. I never drew up a contract, but if I had to do it again I would draw up just a 1 to 2 page letter stating all artwork produced for the purpose of hosting an event with my business I have exclusive rights to. That little piece of paper can hold a lot of weight in court. I would also put their wage in there. Keep it simple.

I hope this has answered your question…
Good Luck….
Anne Ruemler
Spirited Canvases
"Where paint, canvas and great people come together!"

QUESTION #16:

Ms. Ruemler,
Hey there I was interested in your list of suppliers. Also had some questions on the calendar thing do they set up the pages to check out too?

ANNE'S RESPONSE:

Good Evening,
  I found your email in my junk folder. I is always great to hear from fellow entrepreneurs. ... This is a wonderful business and in the right market can earn you a good income.

      I bought most of my supplies at Michaels Crafts. I bought the cheap craft smart paint in different colors to give my painters a choice of colors for their artwork. The paint comes in 2 or 3oz bottles and dries very quickly. Acrylic paint is the only paint I used... easy to clean up with soap and water and dries quickly so your painters don't get bored waiting for a color to dry.
  I did buy half gallon jugs of Black and White. Again I bought that at Michael's crafts. Shipping cost on paint was outrageous.
  You can get a great price on 7 pack canvases also from Michaels. I used 16x20. You just have to do the math to see what sale is the best price.
      I had an artist buy a lot of her inventory from an online store. Www.Jerrysartarama.com. this is a great place for brushes.

  Hope this helps...

The website? I spent an afternoon setting up my WIX website.
  VERY user friendly...then I opened an eBay account for accepting payments. I then gave that information to the guys at cimplebox and they attached the PayPal button and the calendar to my website. Took all of 48 hours!!
  GOOD LUCK! Please let me know how it goes.
Anne Ruemler
Spirited Canvases
"Where paint, canvas and good people come together!"

QUESTION #17:

Anne,

Thanks so much for responding. I hope I didn't seem like I was 'stalkish'. I just wanted to make sure you got my questions and I wasn't in a crowd of emails. I do have two more questions--how did you compete with other paint and sip companies? Just to make sure you had the artist pencil all the canvases. What do you think about Deco art program?
I will definitely add a comment for your book I hope you get rave reviews. Thanks again

ANNE'S RESPONSE:

Good Evening,
 I personally think that competition is good. It gives customers a choice. I think connecting with your painter is key to this business. You must be likable. You must like people. You must be compassionate. Some people come to these events because they are looking for an escape. Some painters just want to experience the next FAD. Some Painters are themselves artists and just want to hang out with likeminded people. Doesn't matter to me why they came to one of my events. I will make DAMN sure they leave with a finished painting and a smile on their face!!

    I did not have my artist pencil the canvases. For the average beach or tree paining we started with a blank canvas. If we were painting a Fleur De Lis or a Derby Hat then yes my artist would trace out the subject.

I am not familiar with the Art Deco Program. It looks promising if you could get involved in it somehow, but in my area we have not explored that yet.

Hope to talk to you soon,
Anne Ruemler
Spirited Canvases
"Where paint, canvas and good people come together!"

QUESTION #18:

Hi how are you Anne I read your book and I loved it!!! So informative. And of course inspiring I am super thrilled to do this. I wanted to ask about venues when you go to restaurants what do you tell them or is there like a format or a process. I am excited to learn.

ANNE'S RESPONSE:

As far as talking with the Restaurant Manager I would just introduce myself and hand them a flyer. Many restaurants are familiar with these types of events and are more than willing to let you host a party there. With that in mind, I created 2 types of flyers.

1. That simply introduced and promoted my business and the different type of events, ie: Birthdays, Girls night out, fundraisers or face painting.

2. An actual event specific to a venue with a picture of the painting, times and prices. I would have venues hand out these flyers the two weeks leading up to the event.

   I found that if I inserted a picture of the actual painting for that event I received more calls. This is a great way to get your name out there. Make sure to add you LOGO and tag line. People remember those.

   Talk to you soon,

   Anne

QUESTION #19:

Anne,

I was wondering if you could give me some more information on your military contract. How did you approach them?

Who do I even contact?

I live close to a military base and would love to host events for our troops also. Thank you, G.

ANNE'S RESPONSE:

Okay, now to the Military contract. I was very fortunate to have at one time worked with a lady that managed events for the soldiers and families.

When approaching the MWR (Morale Welfare and Recreation) on base, which can be done with a phone call if necessary, simply ask to speak to the Coordinator for events, then take in a couple paintings and a great flyer with pricing, and introduce yourself. The trend has been around long enough now, many in the military community are familiar with what it is we do, but if you do meet someone unfamiliar, have them contact Fort Knox MWR or another military post that offers this event, for clarification.

Once you have been approved through the local MWR you will then sign a contract with the United States Government. The next step will be to fill out a W-9 form for tax purposes. I made anywhere from $400-$1000 a month just from one, 2hour event.

This process took about 4 months. Once I was contracted they would ask me to do additional events like face painting for kids or a "Mommy and Me" event on Mother's day. The MWR will do A

TON of advertising for you for FREE. My business just blossomed once I became known on Fort Knox. It was an amazing experience. I hope this has helped answer your questions.

Sincerely, Anne Ruemler

IN SUMMARY

There you go everyone, this brings us to the end of the Questions and Answers. I have tried to answer all my e-mail personally, and have appreciated the opportunity to speak and offer guidance to many others just getting started in their own businesses. This has been a roller coaster year, and truly am grateful for the experience.

I was amazed at all the little details I forgot to put in my original book. This shows me that people are thinking and very passionate about their businesses. I can foresee reaching out to fellow entrepreneurs for many years to come.

I have currently sold over two hundred books and received dozens of emails with questions and encouragement from all over the world. I appreciate each and every one that bought my book. Each question was a new learning curve for me too. Some questions challenged me, and to have some of the answers I had to experience that obstacle and just overcome it myself. I put honesty and experience into my business and so I felt compelled to put honesty and my experience into my books.

I have found that I enjoy writing, though I am not very good at it, however, I do love to talk and teach. I think this is why I like to write about business. I like nonfiction, and subjects that make you think, and challenge the mind. I personally try to learn something new every day. Like I said earlier. Knowledge is power and I love sharing both!

Happy painting!!!

Made in the USA
San Bernardino, CA
11 May 2017